# THE ORIGINS OF TULSI

## A LOOK AT THE MYTHOLOGICAL ROOTS OF THE PLANT

DR. JAGADEESH PILLAI

Made with ♥ on the Notion Press Platform
www.notionpress.com

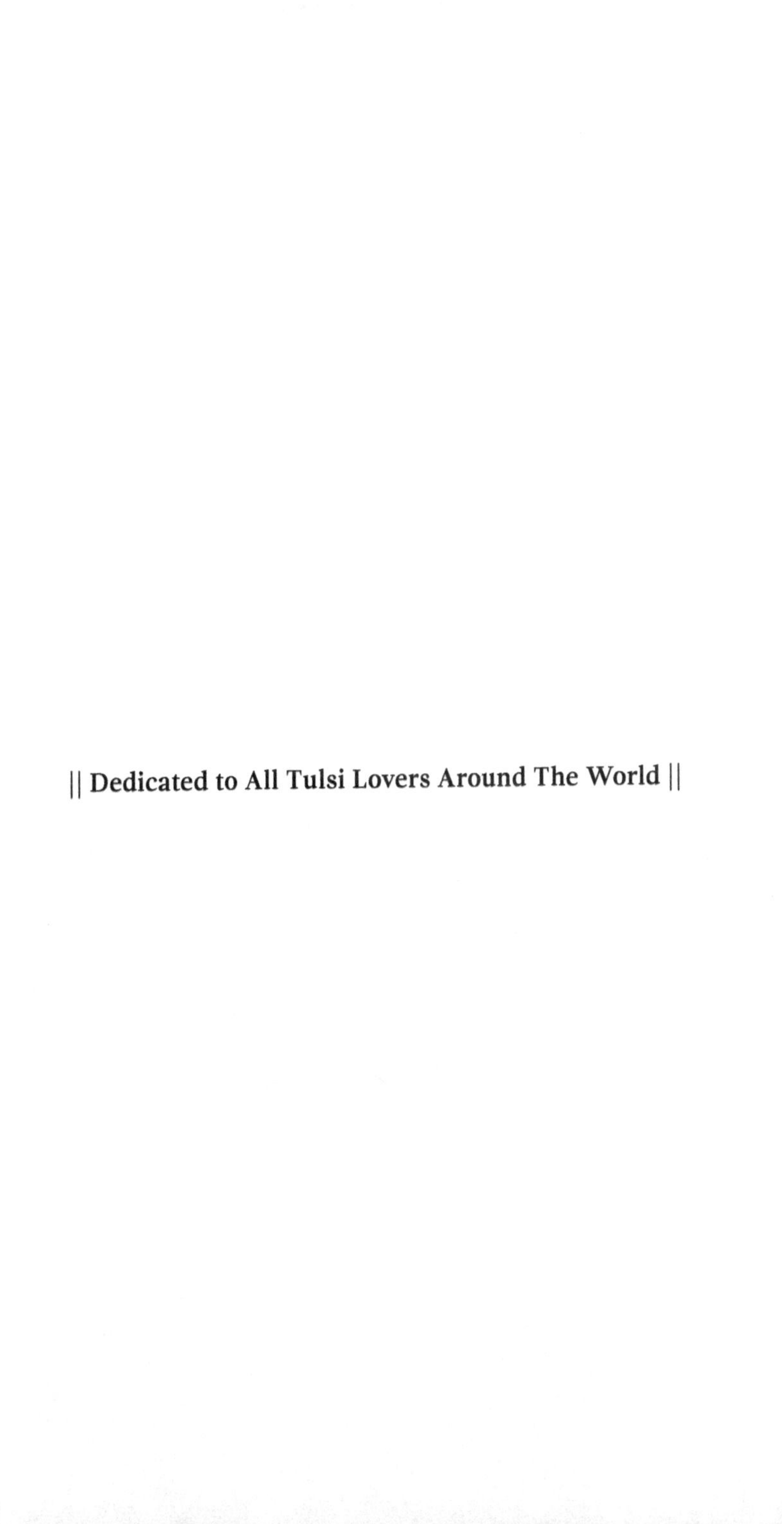

|| Dedicated to All Tulsi Lovers Around The World ||

# Contents

# Contents

# Prayer

**"Om Tulsidevye Cha Vidmahe Vishnupriyaye Cha
Dheemahi Tanno Vrinda Prachodayat"**

*May I meditate on the divine essence of Ocimum, O
Goddess beloved by Vishnu, grant me intellect and
enlightenment, and let Brindha fill my mind with
illumination.*

# About The Author

Dr. Jagadeesh Pillai is a renowned Guinness World Record holder, writer, and researcher hailing from Varanasi, also known as the abode of Lord Shiva. With a Ph.D. in Vedic Science and a range of creative ideas and achievements, he is a true polymath. Although his roots can be traced back to Kerala, the people of Varanasi hold him in high regard and affectionately consider him one of their own.

Dr. Pillai has achieved four Guinness World Records in the following subjects:

1. "Script to Screen" - In this record, Dr. Pillai produced and directed an animation film within the shortest time possible, breaking the previous record set by Canadians. He has also received numerous national and international awards and recognitions for this achievement.

2. Longest Line of Postcards - For this record, Dr. Pillai created a line of 16,300 postcards on the occasion of the 163rd anniversary of Indian Postal Day. The event also included a questionnaire about the Indian flag.

3. Largest Poster Awareness Campaign - Dr. Pillai designed an awareness campaign on the subject of "Beti Bachao - Beti Padhao" (Save the Girl Child - Educate the Girl Child) to achieve this record.

4. Largest Envelope - In tribute to the Indian Prime Minister's "Make in India" initiative, Dr. Pillai created a 4000 square meter envelope using waste paper to achieve this record.

5. Attempted - 70000 Candles on a 210 kg Cake - To celebrate the 70th Indian Independence Day, Dr. Pillai attempted to light 70,000 candles on a 210 kg cake, which was recorded in World Records India.

6. Attempted - Documentary on Dhamek Stupa of Sarnath in 17 Languages - Dr. Pillai attempted to create a documentary on the Dhamek Stupa of Sarnath, dubbing it in 17 different languages. The result of this attempt is currently awaiting confirmation from the Guinness World Records.

He is versatile in Gita teaching. The young generation is fond of his Gita teaching and he has changed the life of many young through his continued motivational boost up and teachings.

He has composed and sung Gayatri Mantra in 1008 different tunes.

He has composed and sung Hanuman Chalisa in 108 different tunes.

He has composed and sung hundreds of Sanskrit Bhajans, Patriotic songs, etc.

He has written and directed so many short films and documentaries for awareness campaigns.

He has done voluntary services to UP Police and Kerala Police to spread awareness campaigns on the various issue through videos and photography.

He is on the path of authoring thousands of books on Indian culture, Indian Temples, and the life of extraordinary people.

It is hard to believe that he has produced and directed more than 100 Documentaries on a particular city (Varanasi) which is done by a single person.

He has helped and guided more than 25 boys and girls to achieve world records through various creative and innovative methods.

A multifaceted person who can apply the best of his intellect using the God-given blessings which have been showered upon every human being granting them an immense capacity to learn, experience, and experiment with many things and do wonders in this world of discrimination and disparities.

He is a teacher and a student at the same time who always learns every day and teaches every day. As a master, his weakness was that he never sticks to a particular subject.

Perhaps this weakness gives him the strength to master any area which he came across.

Each of his days dawned with learning a new topic and he spend most of his time experimenting and researching it.

He is also a selfless social activist and a motivational speaker.

His life was full of struggle, ups and downs, and failures. But he never gave up and faced all his trials and tribulations full of confidence. Today he is a successful young man with a lot of enthusiasm and rich life experience.

He is an efficient Tarot Card Reader, Astro-Vastu Consultant and an excellent singer and composer.

He has sung full Ram Charita Manas 138 hours audio by his own composition. He has also sung the whole Bhagavad-Gita in his own composition with a rhythmic background.

He has also sung "Lokah Samastha Sukhino Bhavantu" in 50 different languages.

Currently working on a detailed and scientific study on Veda, Upanishad, Puranas, Bhagavad Gita, etc.

He has composed and sung Hanuman Chalisa in 108 different compositions and Gayatri Mantra in 1008 different compositions.

**<u>Awards</u>**

Four Times Guinness World Records, Winner of Mahatma Gandhi Vishwa Shanti Puraskar , Mahatma Gandhi Global Peace Ambassador, Kashi Ratna Award, Dr. APJ Abdul Kalam Motivational Person of the Year 2017, Mother Teresa Award, Indira Gandhi Priyadarshini Award, Bharat Vikas Ratna Award, Udyog Ratna Award, Vigyan Prasar Award, Poorvanchal Ratn Samman.

# Preface

The Tulsi plant has been regarded as both mythic and religious across Hindu belief systems for centuries, with many stories attesting to its special spiritual powers. Traditionally seen as the embodiment of the divine mother, Shakti, Tulsi's essence is believed to infuse any place where it is planted. In this book, we will explore both the mythic and religious significance of the sacred Tulsi.

From tales of its origin to common customs observed around it, this book will delve into the unique relationship between Tulsi and Hindu belief systems and practices. For example, we will discuss the ritualistic worship of this plant and how it helps devotees approach their spiritual journeys. Additionally, the stories behind the origin of Tulsi and its many incarnations will be explored, while scientific insights into its properties and uses will also be featured.

Throughout this book, the reader will encounter references to ancient texts, artwork, and scholarly research while tracing the history of Tulsi in Hindu belief systems. Detailing its various forms as a sacred plant to its modern day uses, this book will serve as an informative and inspirational guide to understanding Tulsi and its place within the Hindu faith.

Overall, it is our hope that this book will become a valuable resource for readers, who wish to learn more about Hindu beliefs and attitudes about the sacred plant. It is important to note that the book is in no way meant to be comprehensive story about Hinduism and its relationship with Tulsi, as the religion incorporates a diverse range of ceremonial practices, myths, and rituals. Rather, this book will attempt to expand upon the primary themes and beliefs associated with the Tulsi.

We hope you enjoy this journey into the spiritual and religious world of the Tulsi plant.

# THE ORIGINS OF TULSI: A LOOK AT THE MYTHOLOGICAL ROOTS OF THE PLANT

Tulsi, also known as Ocimum tenuiflorum, holy basil, or tulasi, is an aromatic perennial plant that holds great significance in Hinduism and has a long history of use in traditional medicine. But where did this holy plant come from, and how did it become so revered in Hindu belief and culture?

According to Hindu mythology, Tulsi was a devoted wife named Vrinda who was transformed into a plant by the god Vishnu as punishment for her husband's infidelity. Vrinda's devotion to her husband was so strong that even after her transformation, her devotion to him remained unchanged, and she became known as Tulsi, the "incomparable one."

Tulsi is also said to be an avatar of the goddess Lakshmi, the consort of Vishnu, and is often depicted in Hindu art as a woman with a crown of leaves on her head. In Hindu tradition, the plant is considered to be a symbol of purity and is often planted in the courtyard of homes and temples as a sacred, protective presence.

In addition to its mythological origins, Tulsi has a long history of use in traditional medicine. Ayurveda, the ancient Indian system of medicine, considers Tulsi to be a "rasayana," or a substance that promotes physical and spiritual well-being. The plant is believed to have a number of health benefits, including the ability to reduce stress, improve respiratory function, and boost the immune system.

Tulsi is also considered to be a natural detoxifier and is often used to support the liver and improve digestion. In addition to its medicinal properties, Tulsi is also used in Hindu rituals and ceremonies, such as the puja, or worship of the gods. The plant is often offered to the gods as a symbol of devotion, and its leaves are believed to have the power to purify the mind and body.

Despite its ancient origins and long history of use, Tulsi is still widely cultivated and revered in modern India and around the world. The plant is grown in many parts of Asia, Africa, and South America, and its popularity has spread to other parts of the world through the spread of Hinduism and Ayurveda.

Today, Tulsi is commonly used in a variety of products, including teas, essential oils, and natural beauty and health products. Its popularity continues to grow as more people discover the many benefits of this sacred plant.

In conclusion, Tulsi, or holy basil, is a plant that holds great significance in Hindu mythology and traditional medicine. It is believed to have a number of health benefits and is used in a variety of rituals and ceremonies. Despite its ancient origins, Tulsi remains a popular and revered plant in modern times, with a growing presence in products and practices around the world.

# CHAPTER TWO

# THE ROLE OF TULSI IN HINDU BELIEFS AND PRACTICES

Tulsi, also known as Ocimum tenuiflorum or holy basil, is a plant that holds a special place in Hindu beliefs and practices. In Hindu mythology, Tulsi is considered to be an avatar of the goddess Lakshmi, the consort of Vishnu, and is often depicted in Hindu art as a woman with a crown of leaves on her head.

In Hindu tradition, Tulsi is considered to be a symbol of purity and is often planted in the courtyard of homes and temples as a sacred, protective presence. The plant is believed to have the power to purify the mind and body and is often used in rituals and ceremonies as a symbol of devotion.

One such ceremony is the puja, or worship of the gods,

in which Tulsi leaves are often offered as a symbol of devotion. The leaves are believed to have the power to purify the mind and body and are often used in the puja as a means of creating a connection with the divine.

Tulsi is also believed to have a number of health benefits and is commonly used in traditional medicine, such as Ayurveda. In Ayurveda, Tulsi is considered to be a "rasayana," or a substance that promotes physical and spiritual well-being. The plant is believed to have the ability to reduce stress, improve respiratory function, and boost the immune system.

In addition to its use in traditional medicine, Tulsi is also used in Hindu rituals and ceremonies as a means of purification and protection. The plant is often used to create a sacred space or to protect against negative energy.

In conclusion, Tulsi holds a special place in Hindu beliefs and practices. It is considered to be a symbol of purity and is often used in rituals and ceremonies as a means of devotion and purification. The plant is also believed to have a number of health benefits and is commonly used in traditional medicine.

# CHAPTER THREE

# THE MANY HEALTH BENEFITS OF TULSI: FROM A TO Z

Tulsi, also known as Ocimum tenuiflorum or holy basil, is a plant that has been used for centuries in traditional medicine and is believed to have a number of health benefits. Here are just a few of the many ways that Tulsi can benefit your health:

**A: Adaptogen:** Tulsi is considered to be an adaptogen, meaning that it can help the body adapt to stress and maintain balance.

**B: Boosts the immune system:** Tulsi is believed to have immune-boosting properties and is often used to help prevent illness.

**C: Calms the mind:** Tulsi is thought to have a calming effect on the mind and is often used to reduce stress and anxiety.

**D: Detoxifies the body:** Tulsi is believed to have natural detoxifying properties and is often used to support the liver and improve digestion.

**E: Enhances skin health:** Tulsi is believed to have antibacterial and anti-inflammatory properties and is often used in natural beauty products to improve skin health.

**F: Fights inflammation:** Tulsi is believed to have anti-inflammatory properties and is often used to reduce inflammation in the body.

**G: Good for the heart:** Tulsi is believed to have a positive effect on heart health and is often used to lower blood pressure and cholesterol levels.

**H: Helps with respiratory issues:** Tulsi is believed to have respiratory benefits and is often used to relieve symptoms of colds and allergies.

**I: Improves digestion:** Tulsi is believed to have digestive benefits and is often used to improve digestion and reduce bloating.

**J: Just what you need:** With its many health benefits, Tulsi may be just what you need to improve your overall well-being.

**K: Keeps you healthy:** Tulsi is believed to have a number of health benefits and is often used as a natural way to maintain good health.

**L: Lowers blood sugar levels:** Some research suggests that Tulsi may have the ability to lower blood sugar levels and may be helpful for people with diabetes.

**M: Mood booster:** Tulsi is believed to have a positive effect on mood and is often used to reduce stress and improve mental well-being.

**N: Natural remedy:** With its many health benefits, Tulsi is often used as a natural remedy for a variety of ailments.

**O: Oral health:** Tulsi is believed to have antibacterial properties and is often used in natural oral hygiene products to improve dental health.

**P: Protects against infections:** Tulsi is believed to have antimicrobial properties and is often used to protect against infections.

**Q: Quietens the mind:** Tulsi is believed to have a calming effect on the mind and is often used to improve mental clarity and focus.

**R: Reduces inflammation:** Tulsi is believed to have anti-inflammatory properties and is often used to reduce inflammation in the body.

**S: Supports the immune system:** Tulsi is believed to have immune-boosting properties and is often used to support the immune system.

**T: Traditional medicine:** Tulsi has a long history of use in traditional medicine systems, such as Ayurveda, and is considered to be a "rasayana," or a substance that promotes physical and spiritual well-being.

**U: Unique flavor:** Tulsi has a unique, spicy-sweet flavor that makes it a popular choice for tea and other culinary applications.

**V: Versatile plant:** Tulsi has a wide range of uses, from traditional medicine to natural beauty products to culinary applications.

**W: Well-being:** With its many health benefits, Tulsi may help improve your overall well-being.

**X: eXtraordinary plant:** With its unique flavor and wide range of health benefits, Tulsi is an extraordinary plant that has a special place in traditional medicine and modern wellness practices.

**Y: Youthful skin:** Tulsi is believed to have anti-aging properties and is often used in natural beauty products to improve skin health and appearance.

**Z: Zest for life:** With its many health benefits, Tulsi may help you feel your best and have a greater zest for life.

In conclusion, Tulsi is a plant that has a number of health benefits and has been used for centuries in traditional medicine. From boosting the immune system to fighting inflammation, Tulsi may be a helpful addition to your health routine.

# CHAPTER FOUR

# THE ROLE OF TULSI IN HINDU BELIEFS AND PRACTICES

Tulsi, also known as Ocimum tenuiflorum or holy basil, is a plant that holds a special place in Hindu beliefs and practices. In Hindu mythology, Tulsi is considered to be an avatar of the goddess Lakshmi, the consort of Vishnu, and is often depicted in Hindu art as a woman with a crown of leaves on her head.

In Hindu tradition, Tulsi is considered to be a symbol of purity and is often planted in the courtyard of homes and temples as a sacred, protective presence. The plant is believed to have the power to purify the mind and body and is often used in rituals and ceremonies as a symbol of devotion.

One such ceremony is the puja, or worship of the gods,

in which Tulsi leaves are often offered as a symbol of devotion. The leaves are believed to have the power to purify the mind and body and are often used in the puja as a means of creating a connection with the divine.

Tulsi is also believed to have a number of health benefits and is commonly used in traditional medicine, such as Ayurveda. In Ayurveda, Tulsi is considered to be a "rasayana," or a substance that promotes physical and spiritual well-being. The plant is believed to have the ability to reduce stress, improve respiratory function, and boost the immune system.

In addition to its use in traditional medicine, Tulsi is also used in Hindu rituals and ceremonies as a means of purification and protection. The plant is often used to create a sacred space or to protect against negative energy.

In conclusion, Tulsi holds a special place in Hindu beliefs and practices. It is considered to be a symbol of purity and is often used in rituals and ceremonies as a means of devotion and purification. The plant is also believed to have a number of health benefits and is commonly used in traditional medicine.

# Tulsi in Ayurveda: How the Plant is Used in Traditional Medicine

Ayurveda is an ancient Indian system of medicine that has been practiced for over 5,000 years. In Ayurveda, Tulsi, also known as Ocimum tenuiflorum or holy basil, is considered to be a "rasayana," or a substance that promotes physical and spiritual well-being. The plant is believed to have a number of health benefits and is used in a variety of ways in traditional Ayurvedic medicine.

One of the main ways that Tulsi is used in Ayurveda is as a natural remedy for a variety of ailments. The plant is believed to have immune-boosting, antibacterial, and anti-inflammatory properties and is often used to treat respiratory issues, such as colds and allergies, as well as digestive issues and skin conditions.

Tulsi is also believed to have a calming effect on the mind and is often used to reduce stress and improve mental well-being. The plant is often consumed as a tea or taken in supplement form to support the immune system and improve overall health.

In addition to its medicinal uses, Tulsi is also used in Ayurveda as a natural beauty product. The plant is believed to have anti-aging properties and is often used in natural skin care products to improve skin health and appearance.

Overall, Tulsi is an important plant in Ayurveda and is used in a variety of ways to support physical and spiritual well-being. Its many health benefits make it a popular choice in traditional medicine and modern wellness practices.

# CHAPTER SIX

# "THE CULTURAL SIGNIFICANCE OF TULSI IN INDIA AND AROUND THE WORLD

Tulsi, also known as Ocimum tenuiflorum or holy basil, is a plant that holds great cultural significance in India and around the world. In Hindu mythology, Tulsi is considered to be an avatar of the goddess Lakshmi, the consort of Vishnu, and is often depicted in Hindu art as a woman with a crown of leaves on her head.

In Hindu tradition, Tulsi is considered to be a symbol of purity and is often planted in the courtyard of homes and temples as a sacred, protective presence. The plant is believed to have the power to purify the mind and body and is often used in rituals and ceremonies as a symbol of devotion.

One such ceremony is the puja, or worship of the gods, in which Tulsi leaves are often offered as a symbol of devotion. The leaves are believed to have the power to purify the mind and body and are often used in the puja as a means of creating a connection with the divine.

Tulsi is also an important plant in Ayurveda, the ancient Indian system of medicine, and is considered to be a "rasayana," or a substance that promotes physical and spiritual well-being. The plant is believed to have a number of health benefits and is commonly used in traditional medicine to support the immune system and improve overall health.

In addition to its cultural and medicinal significance, Tulsi is also an important plant in the Hindu belief in reincarnation. In Hindu tradition, it is believed that when a person dies, their soul is reborn in another body, and the Tulsi plant is considered to be a bridge between the physical world and the spiritual world.

Tulsi is also widely cultivated and revered in other parts of Asia, Africa, and South America, where it is used in traditional medicine and in various cultural rituals and ceremonies. The plant's popularity has also spread to other parts of the world through the spread of Hinduism and Ayurveda.

Overall, Tulsi is a plant that holds great cultural significance in India and around the world. Its many uses and benefits make it an important plant in a variety of cultural traditions and practices.

# CHAPTER SEVEN

# "Tulsi and the Environment: How the Plant Can Benefit the Planet"

Tulsi, also known as Ocimum tenuiflorum or holy basil, is a plant that has many benefits not just for humans, but also for the environment. Here are just a few ways that Tulsi can benefit the planet:

Air purification: Tulsi is believed to have natural air-purifying properties and can help to improve indoor air quality.

Pest control: Tulsi has a strong aroma that can help to repel pests, making it a natural alternative to chemical pesticides.

Soil health: Tulsi is a hardy plant that can grow in a variety of soil conditions and can help to improve soil health by adding nutrients to the soil.

Water conservation: Tulsi is a drought-resistant plant that requires minimal watering, making it a great choice for dry climates and areas with water scarcity.

Biodiversity: Tulsi is a nectar-rich plant that attracts a variety of pollinators, such as bees, butterflies, and hummingbirds, which can help to increase biodiversity in the area.

Carbon sequestration: Tulsi is a fast-growing plant that can absorb carbon dioxide from the atmosphere, making it a potential tool for mitigating climate change.

Waste management: Tulsi can be used in waste management systems to help break down organic waste and reduce the amount of landfill waste.

Overall, Tulsi is a plant that has many benefits for the environment. From air purification to carbon sequestration, Tulsi is a valuable addition to any ecosystem.

# CHAPTER EIGHT

# THE VERSATILITY OF TULSI: FROM TEA TO SKIN CARE

Tulsi, also known as Ocimum tenuiflorum or holy basil, is a versatile plant that has a wide range of uses. Here are just a few of the many ways that Tulsi can be used:

Tea: Tulsi is a popular choice for tea due to its unique, spicy-sweet flavor. The plant is believed to have a number of health benefits and is often consumed as a tea to support the immune system and improve overall health.

Essential oils: Tulsi is often used to create essential oils that are used in aromatherapy and natural beauty products. The plant is believed to have calming and stress-reducing properties and is often used to improve mental well-being.

Natural beauty products: Tulsi is believed to have

antibacterial and anti-inflammatory properties and is often used in natural beauty products to improve skin health and appearance. The plant is also believed to have anti-aging properties and is often used in products to help reduce the appearance of fine lines and wrinkles.

Culinary applications: Tulsi is a popular choice for culinary applications due to its unique, spicy-sweet flavor. The plant is often used in Indian cooking and is also used to create herbal infusions and other beverages.

Traditional medicine: Tulsi has a long history of use in traditional medicine systems, such as Ayurveda, and is considered to be a "rasayana," or a substance that promotes physical and spiritual well-being. The plant is believed to have a number of health benefits and is often used to support the immune system and improve overall health.

Religious rituals and ceremonies: In Hindu tradition, Tulsi is considered to be a sacred plant and is often used in religious rituals and ceremonies as a symbol of devotion. The plant is believed to have the power to purify the mind and body and is often used in the puja, or worship of the gods, as a means of creating a connection with the divine.

Home decor: In Hindu culture, Tulsi is often planted in the courtyard of homes and temples as a sacred, protective presence. The plant is considered to be a symbol of purity and is believed to have the power to purify the home.

Overall, Tulsi is a versatile plant that has a wide range of uses, from tea and essential oils to natural beauty products and traditional medicine. Its unique flavor and many health benefits make it a popular choice for a variety of applications.

# CHAPTER NINE

# TULSI AND STRESS MANAGEMENT: HOW THE PLANT CAN HELP YOU RELAX

Tulsi, also known as Ocimum tenuiflorum or holy basil, is a plant that is believed to have a number of health benefits, including the ability to reduce stress and improve mental well-being. Here are just a few ways that Tulsi can help you relax and manage stress:

Tea: Tulsi tea is a popular choice for stress management due to its unique, spicy-sweet flavor and calming effect on the mind. The plant is believed to have a number of health benefits and is often consumed as a tea to reduce stress and improve mental well-being.

Essential oils: Tulsi essential oil is often used in

aromatherapy to help reduce stress and improve mental clarity. The oil is believed to have a calming effect on the mind and is often used in massage, meditation, and other relaxation practices.

Natural beauty products: Tulsi is believed to have stress-reducing properties and is often used in natural beauty products to improve skin health and appearance. The plant is also believed to have anti-aging properties and is often used in products to help reduce the appearance of fine lines and wrinkles.

Traditional medicine: Tulsi is an important plant in Ayurveda, the ancient Indian system of medicine, and is considered to be a "rasayana," or a substance that promotes physical and spiritual well-being. The plant is believed to have a number of health benefits and is often used in traditional medicine to reduce stress and improve mental well-being.

Overall, Tulsi is a plant that has many potential benefits for stress management. Whether consumed as a tea, used in essential oils or natural beauty products, or incorporated into traditional medicine practices, Tulsi may be a helpful tool for reducing stress and improving mental well-being.

# CHAPTER TEN

# THE RELIGIOUS SIGNIFICANCE OF TULSI IN HINDU TEMPLES

Tulsi, also known as Ocimum tenuiflorum or holy basil, is a plant that holds great religious significance in Hinduism and is often found in Hindu temples. In Hindu tradition, Tulsi is considered to be a sacred plant and is believed to have the power to purify the mind and body.

One way that Tulsi is used in Hindu temples is as a symbol of devotion and purity. The plant is often planted in the courtyard of temples and is considered to be a sacred, protective presence. In Hindu mythology, Tulsi is considered to be an avatar of the goddess Lakshmi, the consort of Vishnu, and is often depicted in Hindu art as a woman with a crown of leaves on her head.

Another way that Tulsi is used in Hindu temples is in the

puja, or worship of the gods. During the puja, Tulsi leaves are often offered as a symbol of devotion and are believed to have the power to purify the mind and body. The leaves are also used as a means of creating a connection with the divine.

In addition to its use in religious rituals and ceremonies, Tulsi is also an important plant in Hindu belief in reincarnation. In Hindu tradition, it is believed that when a person dies, their soul is reborn in another body, and the Tulsi plant is considered to be a bridge between the physical world and the spiritual world.

Overall, Tulsi is a plant that holds great religious significance in Hinduism and is often used in Hindu temples as a symbol of devotion and purity. Its many uses and benefits make it an important plant in Hindu religious practices.

# CHAPTER ELEVEN

# Tulsi and Marriage: The Plant's Role in Hindu Weddings

Tulsi, also known as Ocimum tenuiflorum or holy basil, is a plant that holds great significance in Hindu weddings and is often used in various ceremonies and rituals. In Hindu tradition, Tulsi is considered to be a sacred plant and is believed to have the power to purify the mind and body.

One way that Tulsi is used in Hindu weddings is in the haldi ceremony, which is a pre-wedding ritual in which the bride and groom are applied a paste made from turmeric, sandalwood, and other ingredients to their skin. Tulsi leaves are often added to the paste to add a refreshing aroma and to symbolize purity and good fortune.

Tulsi is also often used in the wedding ceremony itself. The plant is often planted in the courtyard of the wedding venue as a symbol of purity and is believed to bring good fortune to the newlyweds. Tulsi leaves are also often included in the wedding garlands, which are worn by the bride and groom as a symbol of their union.

In addition to its use in wedding ceremonies and rituals, Tulsi is also an important plant in Hindu belief in reincarnation. In Hindu tradition, it is believed that when a person dies, their soul is reborn in another body, and the Tulsi plant is considered to be a bridge between the physical world and the spiritual world. This belief adds a further layer of significance to the use of Tulsi in Hindu weddings, as it symbolizes the union of two souls for eternity.

Overall, Tulsi is an important plant in Hindu weddings and is used in a variety of ways to symbolize purity, good fortune, and the eternal union of two souls. Its many uses and benefits make it a valuable addition to Hindu wedding ceremonies and rituals.

# CHAPTER TWELVE

# TULSI AND SPIRITUALITY: HOW THE PLANT CAN ENHANCE YOUR PRACTICE

Tulsi, also known as Ocimum tenuiflorum or holy basil, is a plant that is often used in spiritual practices and is believed to have the power to enhance spirituality. Here are just a few ways that Tulsi can be used to enhance your spiritual practice:

Meditation: Tulsi is believed to have a calming effect on the mind and is often used in meditation to improve mental clarity and focus. The plant is also believed to have stress-reducing properties and may be helpful in reducing distractions and promoting a sense of inner peace.

Rituals and ceremonies: In Hindu tradition, Tulsi is

considered to be a sacred plant and is often used in rituals and ceremonies as a symbol of devotion. The plant is believed to have the power to purify the mind and body and is often used in the puja, or worship of the gods, as a means of creating a connection with the divine.

Aromatherapy: Tulsi is often used to create essential oils that are used in aromatherapy to promote relaxation and improve mental well-being. The plant is believed to have a calming and stress-reducing effect on the mind and is often used in massage, meditation, and other relaxation practices.

Traditional medicine: Tulsi is an important plant in Ayurveda, the ancient Indian system of medicine, and is considered to be a "rasayana," or a substance that promotes physical and spiritual well-being. The plant is believed to have a number of health benefits and is often used in traditional medicine to support the immune system and improve overall health and well-being.

Overall, Tulsi is a plant that has many potential benefits for spirituality and spiritual practice. Its unique flavor, calming effect on the mind, and many health benefits make it a popular choice for a variety of spiritual practices.

# CHAPTER THIRTEEN

# "Tulsi and Grief: How the Plant Can Help You Heal"

Tulsi, also known as Ocimum tenuiflorum or holy basil, is a plant that is believed to have a number of health benefits, including the ability to help with grief and emotional healing. Here are just a few ways that Tulsi can be used to help with grief:

Tea: Tulsi tea is a popular choice for those dealing with grief due to its unique, spicy-sweet flavor and calming effect on the mind. The plant is believed to have a number of health benefits and is often consumed as a tea to reduce stress and improve mental well-being.

Essential oils: Tulsi essential oil is often used in aromatherapy to help reduce stress and improve mental clarity. The oil is believed to have a calming effect on the mind and is often used in massage, meditation, and other relaxation practices to help with emotional healing.

Traditional medicine: Tulsi is an important plant in Ayurveda, the ancient Indian system of medicine, and is considered to be a "rasayana," or a substance that promotes physical and spiritual well-being. The plant is believed to have a number of health benefits and is often used in traditional medicine to support the immune system and improve overall health and well-being.

Spiritual practices: In Hindu tradition, Tulsi is considered to be a sacred plant and is often used in spiritual practices as a symbol of devotion. The plant is believed to have the power to purify the mind and body and is often used in the puja, or worship of the gods, as a means of creating a connection with the divine.

Overall, Tulsi is a plant that has many potential benefits for those dealing with grief. Its unique flavor, calming effect on the mind, and many health benefits make it a popular choice for those seeking emotional healing and support.

# CHAPTER FOURTEEN

# TULSI AND PREGNANCY: THE PLANT'S ROLE IN AYURVEDIC MEDICINE

Tulsi, also known as Ocimum tenuiflorum or holy basil, is an important plant in Ayurveda, the ancient Indian system of medicine, and is often used to support pregnancy and childbirth. Here are just a few ways that Tulsi is used in Ayurvedic medicine for pregnancy:

Morning sickness: Tulsi is believed to have digestive and nausea-reducing properties and is often used to help alleviate morning sickness.

Immune support: Tulsi is believed to have immune-boosting properties and is often used to support the immune system during pregnancy.

Stress reduction: Tulsi is believed to have stress-reducing properties and is often used to help manage stress during pregnancy.

Pain management: Tulsi is believed to have pain-relieving properties and is often used in traditional medicine to help manage pain during childbirth.

Postpartum support: Tulsi is believed to have a number of health benefits and is often used in traditional medicine to support postpartum recovery and improve overall health and well-being.

Overall, Tulsi is an important plant in Ayurvedic medicine and is often used to support pregnancy and childbirth. Its many health benefits make it a valuable addition to traditional medicine practices for pregnancy and postpartum care.

# CHAPTER FIFTEEN

# TULSI AND DIABETES: HOW THE PLANT CAN HELP CONTROL BLOOD SUGAR LEVELS

Tulsi, also known as Ocimum tenuiflorum or holy basil, is a plant that is believed to have a number of health benefits, including the ability to help control blood sugar levels in those with diabetes. Here are just a few ways that Tulsi can be used to help with diabetes:

Tea: Tulsi tea is a popular choice for those with diabetes due to its unique, spicy-sweet flavor and potential blood sugar-lowering effects. The plant is believed to have a number of health benefits and is often consumed as a tea to support overall health and well-being.

Traditional medicine: Tulsi is an important plant in Ayurveda, the ancient Indian system of medicine, and is considered to be a "rasayana," or a substance that promotes physical and spiritual well-being. The plant is believed to have a number of health benefits and is often used in traditional medicine to support the immune system and improve overall health and well-being.

Supplementation: Tulsi is available in supplement form and is often used to support blood sugar control in those with diabetes.

Diet: Tulsi is a low-calorie, low-carbohydrate plant that may be beneficial for those with diabetes who are trying to manage their blood sugar levels through diet.

Overall, Tulsi is a plant that has many potential benefits for those with diabetes, including the ability to help control blood sugar levels. Its unique flavor, many health benefits, and availability in various forms make it a popular choice for those seeking natural ways to manage diabetes.

# CHAPTER SIXTEEN

# Tulsi and Heart Health: The Plant's Role in Reducing Cardiovascular Risk

Tulsi, also known as Ocimum tenuiflorum or holy basil, is a plant that is believed to have a number of health benefits, including the ability to improve heart health and reduce the risk of cardiovascular disease. Here are just a few ways that Tulsi can be used to support heart health:

Tea: Tulsi tea is a popular choice for those seeking to improve heart health due to its unique, spicy-sweet flavor and potential cardiovascular benefits. The plant is believed to have a number of health benefits and is often consumed as a tea to support overall health and well-being.

Traditional medicine: Tulsi is an important plant in Ayurveda, the ancient Indian system of medicine, and is considered to be a "rasayana," or a substance that promotes physical and spiritual well-being. The plant is believed to have a number of health benefits and is often used in traditional medicine to support the immune system and improve overall health and well-being.

Supplementation: Tulsi is available in supplement form and is often used to support heart health and reduce the risk of cardiovascular disease.

Diet: Tulsi is a low-calorie, low-fat plant that may be beneficial for those seeking to improve heart health through diet.

Overall, Tulsi is a plant that has many potential benefits for heart health and the reduction of cardiovascular risk. Its unique flavor, many health benefits, and availability in various forms make it a popular choice for those seeking natural ways to support heart health.

# CHAPTER SEVENTEEN

# Tulsi and Cancer: The Plant's Potential as a Complementary Therapy

Tulsi, also known as Ocimum tenuiflorum or holy basil, is a plant that is believed to have a number of health benefits and is often used as a complementary therapy in cancer treatment. Here are just a few ways that Tulsi can be used as a complementary therapy in cancer treatment:

Tea: Tulsi tea is a popular choice for those undergoing cancer treatment due to its unique, spicy-sweet flavor and potential health benefits. The plant is believed to have a number of health benefits and is often consumed as a tea to support overall health and well-being.

Traditional medicine: Tulsi is an important plant in Ayurveda, the ancient Indian system of medicine, and is considered to be a "rasayana," or a substance that promotes physical and spiritual well-being. The plant is believed to have a number of health benefits and is often used in traditional medicine to support the immune system and improve overall health and well-being.

Supplementation: Tulsi is available in supplement form and is often used as a complementary therapy in cancer treatment to support overall health and well-being.

Diet: Tulsi is a low-calorie, low-fat plant that may be beneficial for those undergoing cancer treatment who are seeking to support their health through diet.

Overall, Tulsi is a plant that has many potential benefits as a complementary therapy in cancer treatment. Its unique flavor, many health benefits, and availability in various forms make it a popular choice for those seeking natural ways to support their health during cancer treatment.

# TULSI AND IMMUNITY: HOW THE PLANT CAN BOOST YOUR BODY'S DEFENSES

Tulsi, also known as Ocimum tenuiflorum or holy basil, is a plant that is believed to have a number of health benefits, including the ability to boost the immune system and improve overall health and well-being. Here are just a few ways that Tulsi can be used to boost immunity:

Tea: Tulsi tea is a popular choice for those seeking to boost their immune system due to its unique, spicy-sweet flavor and potential health benefits. The plant is believed to have a number of health benefits and is often consumed as a tea to support overall health and well-being.

Traditional medicine: Tulsi is an important plant in

Ayurveda, the ancient Indian system of medicine, and is considered to be a "rasayana," or a substance that promotes physical and spiritual well-being. The plant is believed to have a number of health benefits and is often used in traditional medicine to support the immune system and improve overall health and well-being.

Supplementation: Tulsi is available in supplement form and is often used to support immune function and improve overall health and well-being.

Diet: Tulsi is a low-calorie, low-fat plant that may be beneficial for those seeking to boost their immune system through diet.

Overall, Tulsi is a plant that has many potential benefits for immune health. Its unique flavor, many health benefits, and availability in various forms make it a popular choice for those seeking natural ways to support their immune system.

# CHAPTER NINETEEN

# TULSI AND BEAUTY: THE PLANT'S ROLE IN NATURAL SKIN CARE

Tulsi, also known as Ocimum tenuiflorum or holy basil, is a plant that is believed to have a number of health benefits and is often used in natural skin care products. Here are just a few ways that Tulsi can be used for beauty:

Oil: Tulsi oil is often used in natural skin care products due to its unique, spicy-sweet aroma and potential skin-benefitting properties. The oil is believed to have a number of health benefits and is often used in massage, meditation, and other relaxation practices to support overall health and well-being.

Creams and lotions: Tulsi is often included as an ingredient in natural creams and lotions due to its potential skin-benefitting properties. The plant is believed to have a number of health benefits and is often used in traditional medicine to support overall health and well-being.

Facial masks: Tulsi is often included as an ingredient in natural facial masks due to its potential skin-benefitting properties. The plant is believed to have a number of health benefits and is often used in traditional medicine to support overall health and well-being.

Soaps: Tulsi is often included as an ingredient in natural soaps due to its unique, spicy-sweet aroma and potential skin-benefitting properties.

Overall, Tulsi is a plant that has many potential benefits for beauty and skin care. Its unique aroma, many health benefits, and availability in various forms make it a popular choice for those seeking natural ways to support the health and appearance of their skin.

# CHAPTER TWENTY

# TULSI AND COOKING: DELICIOUS RECIPES FEATURING THE HOLY PLANT

Tulsi, also known as Ocimum tenuiflorum or holy basil, is a plant that is believed to have a number of health benefits and is often used in cooking to add flavor and nutrition to dishes. Here are just a few delicious recipes featuring Tulsi:

Tulsi tea: To make Tulsi tea, simply steep a few Tulsi leaves in hot water for a few minutes and sweeten with honey or sugar to taste.

Tulsi rice: To make Tulsi rice, simply cook rice according

to package instructions and stir in a handful of fresh Tulsi leaves towards the end of the cooking process.

Tulsi chutney: To make Tulsi chutney, blend together equal parts Tulsi leaves, cilantro, and mint with a few cloves of garlic, a squeeze of lemon juice, and enough water to create a smooth consistency.

Overall, Tulsi is a versatile plant that can be used in a variety of dishes to add flavor and nutrition. Its unique, spicy-sweet flavor makes it a delicious and healthy addition to many recipes.

# CHAPTER TWENTY-ONE

# TULSI AND THE FUTURE: THE PLANT'S POTENTIAL FOR A SUSTAINABLE AND HEALTHY WORLD

Tulsi, also known as Ocimum tenuiflorum or holy basil, is a plant that is believed to have a number of health benefits and has the potential to play a significant role in creating a more sustainable and healthy future. Here are just a few ways that Tulsi can contribute to a more sustainable and healthy world:

Environmental benefits: Tulsi is a hardy plant that requires little water and is resistant to pests, making it an environmentally-friendly choice for cultivation. In addition, the plant is believed to have a number of environmental benefits, including the ability to improve soil quality and reduce air pollution.

Health benefits: Tulsi is believed to have a number of health benefits and is often used in traditional medicine to support overall health and well-being. As more people turn towards natural remedies to support their health, Tulsi has the potential to play a significant role in improving global health and well-being.

Sustainable agriculture: Tulsi is a plant that can be grown sustainably, with many small farmers relying on the plant as a source of income. As such, the cultivation of Tulsi has the potential to support sustainable agriculture and provide economic benefits to communities around the world.

Overall, Tulsi is a plant that has the potential to contribute to a more sustainable and healthy future. Its many health benefits, environmental benefits, and potential for sustainable agriculture make it a valuable plant for the future.

# CHAPTER TWENTY-TWO

# TULSI AND THE ARTS: HOW THE PLANT HAS INSPIRED POETRY, MUSIC, AND ART

Tulsi, also known as Ocimum tenuiflorum or holy basil, is a plant that is believed to have a number of health benefits and has inspired a variety of artistic works throughout history. Here are just a few ways that Tulsi has inspired the arts:

Poetry: Tulsi has been the subject of many poems throughout history, with poets often extolling the plant's virtues and spiritual significance.

Music: Tulsi has inspired a variety of musical works, including songs and instrumental pieces that celebrate the plant's beauty and spiritual significance.

Art: Tulsi has been depicted in a variety of artistic works, including paintings, sculptures, and other visual art forms.

Literature: Tulsi has been mentioned in a variety of literature, including religious texts, poetry, and other works that explore the plant's spiritual significance and health benefits.

Overall, Tulsi is a plant that has inspired a variety of artistic works throughout history. Its unique beauty, many health benefits, and spiritual significance make it a popular subject for artistic expression.

# The Other Books Of The Author

1. The Moments When I Met God
2. Kashiyile Theertha Pathangal
3. GURU GYAN VANI
4. Abhiprerak Gita
5. ASSI SE JAIN GHAT TAK
6. Hopelessness of Arjuna
7. The Soul and It's True Nature
8. Sense of Action (Karma)
9. Action through Wisdom
10. Action through Wisdom
11. THEORY AND PRACTICAL OF EVERY ACTION
12. LOGICAL UNDERSTANDING OF THE SUPREME
13. THE IMPERISHABLE SUPREME
14. Yatra Nishadraj se Hanuman Ghat Tak
15. Yatra Karnatak Ghat se Raja Ghat Tak
16. Yatra Pandey Ghat se Prayagraj Ghat Tak
17. Yatra Ranjendra Prasad Ghat se Dattatreya Ghat Tak
18. YaatraSindhiya Ghat se Gwaliar Ghat Tak
19. Yatra Mangala Gauri Ghat se Hanuman Gadhi Ghat Tak
20. Yatra Gaay Ghat Se Nishad Ghat Tak
21. MAA GANGA, GHATEN EVM UTSAV
22. Ganga Arti Dev Deepavali evam Any Utsav
23. Potentials of Digitalized India
24. VEDIC CONSCIOUSNESS
25. A Brief Introduction to Vedic Science
26. Kashi ke Barah Jyotirling
27. IMPACT OF MOTIVATION
28. Let's have a Milky Way Journey
29. Color Therapy in a Nutshell

59. "The Holistic Cow: A Look at the Physical, Spiritual, and Cultural Importance of Cows in India"

# Contact

DR. JAGADEESH PILLAI

PhD in Vedic Science

Four Times Guinness World Record Holder

Winner of Mahatma Gandhi Vishwa Shanti Puraskar and
Global Peace Ambassador

Gemology, Astro & Vastu Consultant - Spiritual Counselor

Consultant for designing World Record Ideas

Efficient Tarot Card Reader

9839093003

myrichindia@gmail.com

drjagadeeshpillai@facebook

drjagadeeshpillai@instagram

jagadeeshpillai@youtube

www. JAGADEESHPILLAI.com

|| LOKAHA SAMASTHAHA SUKHINO BHAVANTU ||